# The Digestive System

## Injury, Illness and Health

Carol Ballard

Heinemann LIBRARY

**www.heinemann.co.uk/library**
Visit our website to find out more information about **Heinemann Library** books.

To order:
☎ Phone 44 (0) 1865 888066
▤ Send a fax to 44 (0) 1865 314091
▥ Visit the Heinemann Bookshop at www.heinemann.co.uk/library to browse our catalogue and order online.

First published in Great Britain by Heinemann Library, Halley Court, Jordan Hill, Oxford OX2 8EJ, part of Harcourt Education.

Heinemann is a registered trademark of Harcourt Education Ltd.

Editorial: Nick Hunter and Catherine Clarke
Design: Jo Hinton-Malivoire and
Tinstar Design Limited  (www.tinstar.co.uk)
Illustrations: Art Construction except pp. 4, 15 by Ken Vail Graphic Design and p. 12 by Geoff Ward
Picture Research: Maria Joannou and
Su Alexander
Production: Viv Hichens

Originated by Ambassador Litho Ltd
Printed and bound in Hong Kong, China by South China Printing Company

ISBN 0 431 15717 0
07 06 05 04 03
10 9 8 7 6 5 4 3 2 1

**British Library Cataloguing in Publication Data**
Ballard, Carol
Digestive System. – (Body focus)
612.3
A full catalogue record for this book is available from the British Library.

**Acknowledgements**
The publishers would like to thank the following for permission to reproduce photographs: Corbis, p. **16**, Corbis Stock Market (Michael Heron) p. **41**; Gareth Boden p. **9**; Getty Images (UHB Trust)p. **14**; Photodisc p. **10**; Rex Features p. **34**; Science Photo Library pp. **17** (Mehau Kulyk), **20** (J. C. Revy), **23** (Biophoto Associates), **24**, **26** (Science Pictures), **27** (David M. Martin), **29** (Professor P. Motta, Dept. of Anatomy, University "La Sapienza"), **30**, **31** (Department of Clinical Radiology, Salisbury District Hospital), **32**, **33**, **35** (Saturn Stills), **40** (Richard J. Green).

Cover photograph of a coloured X-ray, showing the inside of the intestines, reproduced with permission of Science Photo Library.

The publishers would like to thank David Wright for his assistance with the preparation of this book.

Every effort has been made to contact copyright holders of any material reproduced in this book. Any omissions will be rectified in subsequent printings if notice is given to the publishers.

# CONTENTS

Words appearing in the text in bold, **like this**, are explained in the Glossary.

# THE DIGESTIVE SYSTEM

Our bodies cannot make use of the food we eat until it is broken down into smaller, **soluble** particles. This breaking down process is called **digestion**, and the organs that carry it out are called the digestive system. The process happens automatically whenever we eat. Food is broken down, the particles of food are absorbed into the blood and waste is removed from the body.

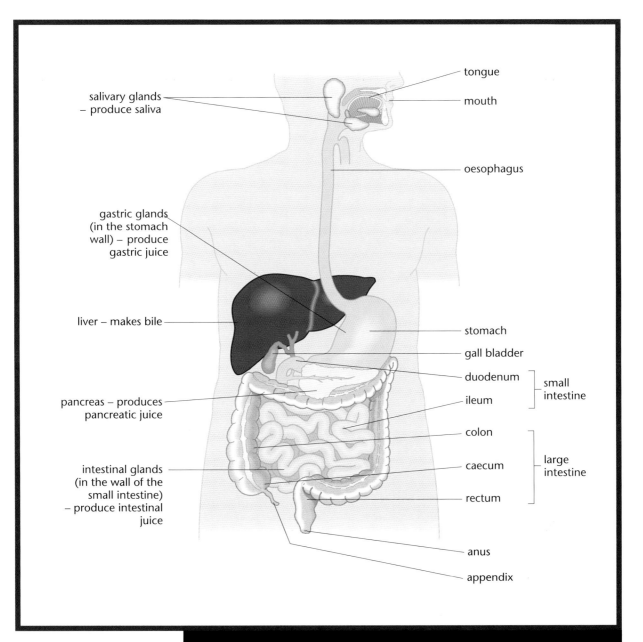

salivary glands – produce saliva

tongue

mouth

oesophagus

gastric glands (in the stomach wall) – produce gastric juice

liver – makes bile

stomach

gall bladder

duodenum — small intestine

pancreas – produces pancreatic juice

ileum

colon

intestinal glands (in the wall of the small intestine) – produce intestinal juice

caecum — large intestine

rectum

anus

appendix

The digestive system processes the food we eat so that our bodies can make use of the chemicals the food contains. This picture shows the main parts of the digestive system and other organs that are involved with the digestive process.

Food gives us energy, the building blocks for growth and repair, as well as the chemicals the body needs to stay fit and healthy. Eating the right amounts of the right types of food is important – eating too much, or too little food can lead to health problems. Not eating a particular food type can also cause problems.

The digestive system is made up of a continuous tube from mouth to **anus** (called the alimentary canal) and other related organs. The alimentary canal begins with the teeth as we bite into our food. The teeth mash the food, and a liquid (**saliva**) in the mouth begins to digest it. Our sense of smell helps us to identify and savour what we are eating, and to alert us to food that may be harmful. Our tongue contains millions of taste buds that allow us to distinguish many different flavours.

When we swallow, the soft food passes into a pipe called the oesophagus, which carries it down to the stomach. Digestive juices in the stomach attack the food, breaking it down even more. The food, which is now a liquid, passes into a long, narrow tube called the small intestine. Here, more juices are added from the small intestine, liver and **pancreas**. The particles that our body can use are absorbed into the blood, which carries them to every part of the body. Waste passes into the large intestine, where water is absorbed into the bloodstream and the waste becomes drier and more solid. This solid waste, called **faeces**, is stored in the rectum until we go to the toilet – when it leaves the body via the anus.

Although not directly involved in digestion, other organs are important in processing the food we eat. The liver regulates the levels of sugars and other chemicals in the blood. The kidneys clean the blood, filtering out any waste chemicals and excess water. The bladder stores the liquid waste, called urine, until we go to the toilet – when the urine leaves the body via a narrow tube called the urethra.

## Physical and chemical digestion

Your food is digested in two main ways:
- physical digestion happens when food is broken into smaller pieces by your teeth and tongue. Food is also broken down by muscles, which push it down the alimentary canal.
- chemical digestion happens when enzymes and other chemicals break down the food at various stages, starting with the saliva in the mouth. This process is made easier because the food has been broken into smaller pieces by physical digestion.

The parts of food that our bodies can use are called **nutrients**. Different foods provide different nutrients. To stay healthy, we need to eat a variety of foods, in the right proportions, providing all the nutrients that we need – a balanced diet.

We can divide foods into six main groups:
*Bread, pasta, rice, flour and cereals*: these foods contain **carbohydrates**, either as starches or as sugars. Unrefined carbohydrates, such as wholegrain cereals and wholemeal flour, also contain fibre, which helps the digestive system to function properly. They are of more value to the body than refined carbohydrates such as white flour and white sugar, which contain little or no fibre. Our bodies use carbohydrates for energy.

*Vegetables*: these are important sources of **vitamins** and **minerals**, which are needed to maintain general good health. For example, vitamin A is needed for healthy skin and hair, and iron is needed for red blood cells to carry oxygen efficiently. Calcium, found in some leafy vegetables, is important for growth and maintenance of strong, healthy teeth and bones. Vegetables also provide fibre, which has no nutritional value, but is important in helping the digestive system to work efficiently. Fibre is the cellulose material that plant cell walls are made of. We are not able to **digest** this, so it adds bulk to the **faeces** and makes it softer – helping it to pass out of the body more quickly. Lack of fibre in the diet can lead to bowel problems.

*Fruits*: these are also important sources of vitamins and minerals. Citrus fruits, such as oranges and grapefruits, are rich in vitamin C, which helps to boost the **immune system**. Like vegetables, fruits contain fibre, which helps the digestive system to function efficiently.

*Dairy products such as milk, yoghurt, butter, and cheese*: these are rich in **fats** that we use for energy. One gram of fat will give about 40 kilojoules of energy. Dairy products are also good sources of calcium, as well as vitamins and **proteins**.

fats, oils & sweets (use sparingly)

milk, yoghurt, & cheese group (2–3 servings)

vegetable group (3–5 servings)

meat, poultry, fish, dry beans, eggs & nuts group (2–3 servings)

fruit group (2–4 servings)

bread, cereal, rice & pasta group (6–11 servings)

Today, most doctors suggest that we should try to get most of our energy from starchy foods such as bread, pasta and rice, and avoid eating a lot of sugar and fat. Think of our daily food intake as a pyramid: eat plenty of the bottom layers, less of the middle layers and little of the top layers!

| Foods for energy | Food | Energy – kJ in 100g |
|---|---|---|
| Energy is measured in units called kilojoules (kJ). We need to balance the amount of energy we use with the amount of energy we get from our food. Some foods contain more energy than others. This table compares the amount of energy in 100 grams of different types of food. | Apple | 201 |
| | Pasta | 563 |
| | Chicken | 662 |
| | Cheese | 1700 |
| | Chocolate | 2070 |
| | Salted Peanuts | 2497 |
| | Butter | 3006 |

*Meat, fish, eggs, nuts and pulses*: these foods are good sources of proteins, which our bodies need for growing and for repairing damage. Proteins are made from smaller units called **amino acids**. The human body cannot make amino acids, but we can change some amino acids into others. However, there are at least eight amino acids (called essential amino acids) that we cannot make in this way and so we have to obtain them from our food. It is easy to obtain all of them from animal sources, but vegetarians have to make sure that they eat a wide variety of different protein foods, as few of them contain all the essential amino acids.

*Fats and oils*: these are found naturally in many foods and we often also add them to foods when serving or cooking. Some meats are very fatty and cooking oils and many dairy products, such as butter, contain very little other than fat. These are good sources of energy and also provide important chemicals that the body needs for a variety of purposes. However, eating a lot of fatty food is bad for us, because the body stores excess fat.

Another vital part of a balanced diet is water. About 60–70 per cent of a human body is water and, although we can survive for several weeks without food, we can only survive a few days without water.

## Malnutrition

Malnutrition occurs when a diet has not provided sufficient proteins or energy for a prolonged time. With too little protein and calories, sufferers show muscle wasting and impaired growth. A diet rich in carbohydrates but lacking in protein leads to a swollen abdomen and muscle wasting. Both types of malnutrition are common in children from areas of the world affected by famine.

# CHEMICAL DIGESTION

**Digestion** is the process of breaking down food into smaller particles that can be used by the body. Different foods are digested in different ways, and in different parts of the digestive system. Food is digested physically into smaller pieces when we chew. As the food passes through the digestive system, chemicals digest the food into separate particles.

## Enzymes

**Enzymes** are **proteins** that make chemical reactions happen. They act as catalysts – speeding up the reactions – but they do not get used up themselves. One enzyme can be used over and over again. Each enzyme is specific – it can only do one job.

Digestive enzymes break down large food **molecules** into much smaller units. There is a different type of enzyme for each type of food molecule. Enzyme names end with 'ase', and the name usually gives some clue about what the enzyme does – for example; a *prot*ease breaks down *prot*eins.

## Proteins

Proteins are found in meats, fish, eggs and nuts. They are very large molecules, made up of smaller units called **amino acids**. There are about 20 different amino acids in animal proteins. A small protein molecule might contain about 100 amino acid molecules, arranged in its own special order.

This table shows where different enzymes are produced in the body, what they act on, and the molecules that are produced by this action.

## Protein digestion

Breakdown of proteins into single amino acids begins in the stomach. A protease enzyme breaks protein molecules down into smaller molecules called peptides. The **pancreas**, an organ that lies below the stomach, produces a liquid called pancreatic juice. This juice contains several more proteases and peptidases. It is added to the partly digested food in the small intestine and its enzymes help to break down the peptides into individual amino acids.

| Type of enzyme | Produced by | Action |
|---|---|---|
| amylase | salivary glands in mouth, pancreas | starch ➔ maltose ➔ glucose |
| protease and peptidase | stomach and pancreas | proteins ➔ peptides ➔ amino acids |
| lipase | pancreas | fats ➔ fatty acids + glycerol |

## Carbohydrates

**Carbohydrates** are found in foods that contain starch or sugar, such as bread, cereals and pasta. They are made from a simple sugar called **glucose**. Two molecules of glucose joined together make another sugar, called maltose. Lots of glucose molecules can be joined together to make polysaccharides like **glycogen** or starch.

## Carbohydrate digestion

Carbohydrates need to be broken down to give single glucose molecules. The digestion of starch begins in the mouth. **Saliva** contains an enzyme called salivary amylase that acts on starch, and begins to break it down into maltose. When the maltose and any remaining starch reaches the small intestine, it is broken down into molecules of glucose, by pancreatic amylase in pancreatic juice.

## Fats

The scientific name for **fats** and oils is lipids. One molecule of fat is made up from three smaller units, called **fatty acids**, and one unit of glycerol. Different fatty acids make up different fats.

## Fat digestion

In the small intestine, **bile** (a liquid produced by the liver) is added to the partly digested food. Bile contains bile salts that break the fats up into small drops. These small drops are broken down even further by lipase, an enzyme in pancreatic juice, separating the molecules of fatty acids and glycerol.

If our diet does not provide all the **nutrients** we need, or if we eat more than we need, we will not be healthy.

## Obesity

Obesity is the medical term for being very overweight. Although there can be other reasons for obesity, it is usually the result of eating too much and exercising too little. Being obese can lead to health problems, including heart disease and diabetes.

## Body weight

If we take in the same amount of energy as we use, our weight will stay the same. If we take in more energy than we use, our weight will go up as our body stores the extra energy as **fats** or **glycogen**. If we take in less energy than we use, our weight will go down as our body uses up some of its store of fats or glycogen. It is important to try to keep a balance between the amount of food we eat, and the amount of energy we use. Being very overweight or very underweight is bad for our overall health.

## Eating disorders

Two common eating disorders are anorexia nervosa and bulimia. People who suffer from anorexia worry excessively about being overweight – even though they are usually very thin. People suffering from anorexia generally eat very little at meal times, or skip meals altogether. They may try to disguise how little they are eating by piling their plate with foods such as salad, which give them very little energy or **protein**. Friends and family may point out to them that they are already thin and need to eat

Junk food is often very high in fats and carbohydrates. It's fine to eat food like this occasionally, but eating it at every meal could lead to health problems.

## Using energy

Even when we are sleeping, our bodies use energy to maintain vital processes such as heartbeat, breathing, brain function and body temperature. The more active we are, the more energy we use up. The amount of energy food contains is usually measured in kilojoules. In 24 hours, an average teenager might use 12,000 kJ:

| Activity | Hourly energy use | Energy used |
|---|---|---|
| 8 hours asleep | 300 kJ | 2400 kJ |
| 8 hours awake but not active e.g. sitting reading or watching television | 400 kJ | 3200 kJ |
| 8 hours physically active e.g. walking, playing football, swimming | 800 kJ | 6400 kJ |
| | Total energy used | 12,000 kJ |

more – but the anorexic person is unable to believe them and carries on denying themselves food. Anorexics can cause great damage to their bodies. If the body does not get the nutrients it needs, it starts to use up muscle and organ tissue, leading to weakness, organ failure and eventually even death. People with anorexia may need help from a doctor or specialist to re-establish a normal, healthy eating pattern. In severe cases, they may need to spend time at a residential centre or hospital.

People who suffer from bulimia also worry about being overweight. They may eat very little, then have a huge eating binge (bout of overeating), after which they make themselves vomit.

## Vitamin deficiencies

In the 18th century, sailors on long voyages had no fresh fruit or vegetables to eat. Many suffered from a disease called scurvy. It made their gums bleed and their teeth fall out. They became weak, their joints became swollen and they usually died. Eventually it was found that giving them lime juice to drink kept them free from scurvy. Now we know that citrus fruits, such as limes, lemons and oranges, contain high amounts of **vitamin** C – and that this prevents scurvy.

# IN THE MOUTH...

**Digestion** begins when food enters the mouth. Teeth chew and soften food, and it is mixed with **saliva**. The tongue detects different tastes in the mouth.

## Saliva

Saliva is a clear liquid made by the salivary glands in the mouth. There are three pairs of salivary glands in the mouth: one pair high at the sides and two pairs under the tongue. In an adult they produce more than 1 litre of saliva every day.

Saliva is neutral or slightly **alkaline**; this means that it is a base (the opposite of an **acid**) and can neutralize acids. Saliva helps to stop tooth decay by neutralizing the acids produced by **bacteria** in the mouth, preventing them damaging the teeth. It also helps to keep the mouth moist and comfortable. It is about 99 per cent water, but also contains **mucus**, mineral salts and the **enzyme** salivary amylase. The mucus helps to make the food slippery and easy to swallow, and the salivary amylase begins the process of starch digestion.

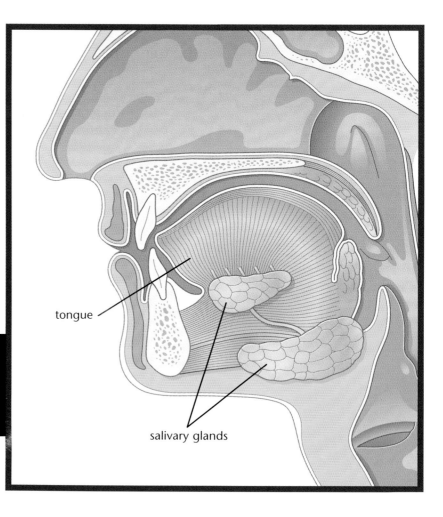

tongue

salivary glands

In this diagram of the inside of the mouth, you can see the positions of the salivary glands.

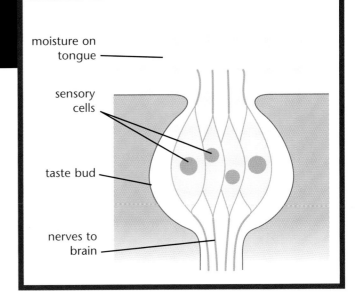

moisture on tongue ──────

sensory cells

taste bud ─

nerves to brain ──────

## Taste

The tongue is mainly muscle. It helps to move food around the mouth when we chew, and it allows us to detect the different tastes of our food. In the upper surface of the tongue, taste-sensitive cells are clustered together in small groups called taste buds. As we chew, chemicals from our food touch our taste buds and electrical signals are sent to the brain. There are four main tastes – sweet, salty, sour and bitter – and scientists used to think that each taste bud could detect only one of these tastes. Recent research shows that it is not quite as simple as that: each taste bud can in fact detect more than one taste, but some areas of the tongue seem to be more sensitive to one type of taste than others. The tip of the tongue is most sensitive to sweet and salty tastes, the sides are most sensitive to sour tastes and the very back is most sensitive to bitter tastes.

Have you ever noticed that when you have a bad cold, your food seems less tasty than usual? This is because the nose also plays an important role in tasting our food. Cells that are sensitive to smells are situated in the upper lining of the nose. When chemicals in the air pass over the hairs of these cells, electrical signals are sent to the brain, adding information to the signals from the taste buds.

## Swallowing

It can be painful if we swallow very hot or very cold food. As food is chewed, it gradually reaches the temperature of the body. When the food has been mixed with saliva and well chewed, it becomes soft and moist and is eventually ready to swallow. Several things happen:
- a flap of cartilage called the epiglottis blocks off the entrance to the windpipe, preventing food entering the airways
- the soft palate blocks off the entrance to the nasal cavity
- the tongue pushes upwards and backwards against the roof of the mouth, pushing a small lump of food, called a **bolus**, to the back of the mouth.

We choose when we begin to swallow – but when the bolus hits the back of the mouth, swallowing becomes an automatic reaction. The food is forced out of the mouth and into the oesophagus.

Babies are born without teeth. The first set of teeth, called milk teeth, grow during the first year of life. During childhood, these gradually fall out and are replaced by permanent teeth. The last four molars, called wisdom teeth, often do not appear until the late teens; sometimes, they may never appear at all. Our teeth are very important, enabling us to take bites of our food and to chew it ready for swallowing.

## Milk teeth

The first teeth usually begin to appear before a baby is a year old. They continue to appear at the rate of about one pair each month until there are twenty milk teeth altogether – ten in the upper jaw and ten in the lower jaw. During early childhood, the permanent teeth slowly develop inside the gums. Between the ages of about six and twelve years, the permanent teeth are ready to emerge and the milk teeth are lost.

## Permanent teeth

Adults have 32 teeth, 16 in each of the upper and lower jaws. Each tooth has two parts: the crown is the part we see above the gum and the root is hidden inside the gum. If these teeth are lost or damaged, the body cannot replace them.

Different shaped teeth do different jobs:
- incisors at the front of the mouth are sharp and are good at snipping off pieces of food. We use these when taking a bite from a large piece of food such as an apple or biscuit.
- canine teeth at the side of the mouth are pointed, and are good for gripping and tearing food
- premolars and molars at the back of the mouth have large flat surfaces for crushing and grinding. We use these to chew our food, softening it and mixing it with **saliva** ready to be swallowed.

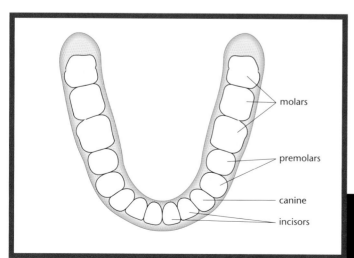

molars

premolars

canine

incisors

## Inside a tooth

Teeth are made up of several layers. The outer layer is a hard, shiny coating called enamel. Beneath this is dentine, a very hard layer like bone. The dentine obtains **nutrients** and oxygen from blood vessels that lie in the pulp (the soft core of the tooth). The pulp also contains nerves.

This diagram shows the positions of the different types of teeth in an adult mouth.

## Teeth and diet

The types of teeth we have give information about our diet. The large, sharp incisors of rodents, such as mice and squirrels, allow them to nibble at their food of nuts and seeds. Carnivores such as lions and foxes have strong canines for gripping and tearing flesh. The flat molars of herbivores, such as sheep and horses, allow them to grind large quantities of plant material. Humans are omnivores and so we have some teeth of each type to enable us to eat a mixed diet

Teeth are not all the same size or shape. Different types of teeth have different functions.

## Looking after teeth

Our permanent teeth should last us for the rest of our lives – but to do this they have to be looked after. It makes sense to:

- remember to clean teeth morning and night, as this helps to remove any scraps of food that remain and eliminate the **bacteria** that cause tooth decay
- avoid sugary, sticky foods, so that there is no sugar remaining on the teeth for harmful bacteria to feed on
- visit the dentist regularly so that any problems are dealt with in the early stages before tooth decay becomes too advanced.

# OESOPHAGUS

The oesophagus – often called the gullet or the foodpipe – carries food from the mouth to the stomach. In an adult it is about 25 centimetres long, and has strong muscular walls that help to move the food along.

The oesophagus is made up of a series of layers. Although there are variations in size and surface details, the basic structure is the same throughout the alimentary canal:

1  the outer layer (adventitia or serosa) is a thin layer of connective tissue
2  beneath this is a layer of **longitudinal muscle** fibres that stretch the full length of the oesophagus
3  next comes a layer of **circular muscle** fibres that run in rings around the oesophagus
4  below this is a thick layer of connective tissue (submucosa) that contains nerves and blood vessels
5  the innermost lining of the oesophagus (**mucosa**) produces **mucus** that keeps the food slippery, helping it to slide easily along.

At the centre is the space through which the food moves – the lumen. Its irregular shape is made by the folds and wrinkles of the mucosa that surround it.

Trained sword swallowers like this one are able to control the natural reflex of the oesophagus muscles, in order to pass the sword into their stomach. Sword swallowing is a life threatening activity and should only be carried out by skilled, trained professionals. NEVER try this yourself.

## Moving food

Food cannot move along by itself. In the oesophagus, muscles contract and relax in turn, pushing the food along. These muscle movements ripple along the oesophagus like a wave. This process is called **peristalsis** and it occurs at every stage along the alimentary canal.

The circular muscles behind the food contract and the circular muscles in front of the food relax. This squeezes the **bolus** along a little way into the space where the muscles are relaxed. These muscles then contract, and the muscles in front relax – squeezing the food along again. The longitudinal muscles contract too, so a section of the oesophagus is shortened, helping to push the bolus forward. Food moves along the oesophagus at about 4 centimetres per second, so it will take about 6 seconds to travel from your mouth to your stomach.

The pressure from the muscles is very high, so food is forced along the digestive system in the right direction – even if you're standing on your head! The bottom of the oesophagus is kept tightly closed by a ring of muscle called the oesophageal **sphincter**. It relaxes to allow food to enter the stomach, and then contracts again to close the entrance to the stomach.

## Wind

With every meal, we swallow air – sometimes as much as half a litre. This may be released from the stomach by belching. Some may enter the small intestine and cause a gurgling sound as it travels along. Any remaining, excess gas leaves the body via the **anus** as flatulence, usually when we go to the toilet.

This patient has swallowed barium meal (a substance that shows up on an X-ray). We can clearly see the tube of the oesophagus (red).

# STOMACH

The stomach stores food from a meal. Digestive juices produced by the stomach break down the food, turning it into a liquid that is then passed on to the rest of the alimentary canal.

The stomach is a muscular sac that stretches to hold food from a meal. An adult's stomach is about 25 centimetres long and is made up of the same layers as the rest of the alimentary canal – a protective outer layer, **longitudinal muscles**, **circular muscles**, connective tissue and **mucosa**. When the stomach is empty, the mucosa becomes wrinkled; as it fills with food. These wrinkles gradually disappear, as the stomach stretches to hold the food.

The mucosa of the stomach contains special glands that make a liquid called **gastric** juice. About 1.5 litres is produced every day. Gastric juice contains:

- pepsin: a type of protease, an **enzyme** that breaks down **proteins** into smaller molecules called peptides
- hydrochloric **acid**: pepsin works best in acidic conditions, so hydrochloric acid is produced to keep the stomach contents acidic. The hydrochloric acid also helps to dissolve **minerals** and kill micro-organisms.

This diagram shows the structure of the stomach wall.

mucosa – inner lining

layer of mucus

gastric glands

submucosa – connective tissue

circular muscle

longitudinal muscle

serosa – protective outer layer

- lipase: this enzyme breaks down **fats** into **fatty acids**. However, because it is inactivated by the hydrochloric acid, little fat digestion takes place in the stomach, but occurs in the small intestine instead.
- mucus: to help to lubricate the food. Mucus also forms a protective layer covering the inside surface of the stomach, preventing it from being attacked by the acid and enzymes of gastric juice.

## Churning food

When food enters the stomach, slow **peristaltic** waves start in the upper area of the stomach, with the muscles of the stomach wall contracting and relaxing about once every 20 seconds. These movements churn the food, mixing it thoroughly with the gastric juice. Different foods stay in the stomach for different lengths of time, depending on the chemicals they contain. Water passes through within a few minutes, a meal rich in **carbohydrates**, such as pasta, may pass through in less than an hour and meals containing fats and proteins, such as steak and chips, may stay in the stomach for 2–3 hours.

The stomach churns and mixes the food, eventually turning it into a creamy liquid called **chyme**. The stomach does not absorb any **nutrients** from the food. The peristaltic movements of the stomach muscles squirt chyme out of the stomach via a ring of muscle, called the pyloric **sphincter**, and into the small intestine.

### Alcohol and the stomach

Alcohol is not a nutrient and may be absorbed into the bloodstream from both the stomach and the small intestine. Absorption is much more rapid from the small intestine, so the longer the alcohol stays in the stomach, the slower the rate of absorption and the lower the level of alcohol in the blood. The stomach also contains an enzyme that breaks down alcohol, so the longer the alcohol stays in the stomach the more it is broken down. Drinking alcohol with a fatty meal such as pizza and chips slows the rate at which alcohol moves into the small intestine, more alcohol is broken down in the stomach and the rate of absorption into the blood is slowed – and so people feel less intoxicated.

# STOMACH PROBLEMS

Everything that we eat and drink passes through the stomach. Our modern diets and lifestyles can sometimes cause stomach problems, although there are often other causes too.

X-rays cannot pass through barium sulphate; if a patient swallows a suspension of barium sulphate (a 'barium meal') the stomach (shown here in yellow/orange) can be seen clearly on an X-ray.

## Stomach ulcers

The thick layer of **mucus** lining the stomach usually protects it from attack by **gastric** juice. Sometimes, however, gastric juice can penetrate the mucus and damage the stomach wall. This damage is called a gastric ulcer. If the damage continues, blood vessels in the stomach wall may rupture, letting blood escape into the stomach. A perforated ulcer occurs if a gastric ulcer eats right through the stomach wall, allowing food and digestive juices to escape into the abdomen.

## What causes ulcers?

There are a variety of factors that may lead to development of a gastric ulcer, although it is unlikely that any of these things would cause an ulcer on its own. They include smoking, drinking a lot of alcohol, eating irregular or hurried meals and stress. All of these things may reduce the stomach's defence and repair mechanisms, making it more susceptible to attack by its own hydrochloric **acid**. Some drugs, such as aspirin, and some steroids may affect the lining of the stomach and increase the risk of developing a gastric ulcer. A **bacterium**, *Helicobacter pylori*, has also been associated with gastric ulcers; it produces **enzymes** that damage the stomach lining.

## Symptoms

A gastric ulcer usually causes pain in the upper abdomen about an hour after a meal. The person may feel sick, and vomiting often helps to relieve the pain. To find out exactly what is wrong, doctors can use an endoscope (a flexible fibre-optic tube that is passed down the throat and into the stomach) to examine the internal walls of the stomach. Alternatively, a barium X-ray can give an indication of the problem. Antacid tablets can ease the pain by neutralizing the stomach acid. A doctor can also prescribe drugs to reduce the amount of stomach acid produced, or to help to form a protective covering over the ulcer. Sometimes an operation is needed to help to repair the damage.

Gastric ulcers that are not treated may eventually begin to bleed, causing **anaemia**. In very severe cases, they can be fatal.

## Indigestion

Usually, the digestive system works without our being aware of it. Sometimes, though, there is pain after eating a meal, together with a bloated, sick feeling. We call this indigestion; it is not dangerous and usually passes after a while.

Several things may cause indigestion. Particular foods, such as curry, onions and cucumber may lead to indigestion. These foods may remain in the stomach for longer than others, producing excess acid. In other cases, it may be due to overeating, eating hurriedly, stress and drinking too much alcohol. Being sick often gets rid of the pain, and antacid tablets can also help.

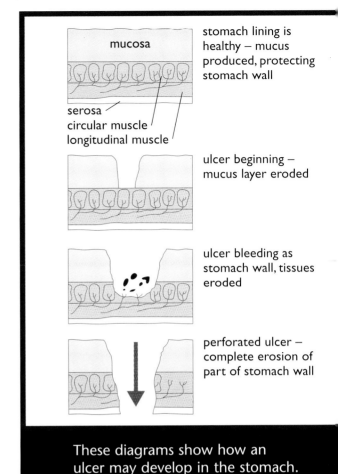

These diagrams show how an ulcer may develop in the stomach.

## Heartburn

The oesophageal **sphincter** usually remains tightly closed to prevent the stomach contents moving back into the oesophagus. Sometimes, however, the acid contents of the stomach do escape into the oesophagus, causing a burning sensation as they irritate the lining of the oesophagus. This is known as heartburn – it is not serious, and antacid tablets can relieve the pain.

## Vomiting

Vomiting is the mechanism by which we can partly, or completely, empty the stomach. Several things happen when we vomit:

- the top of the stomach goes into spasm and **peristaltic** waves start to operate in reverse, pushing food backwards the wrong way along the alimentary canal
- the body of the stomach and the oesophageal sphincter relax
- the upper part of the small intestine also goes into spasm, forcing its contents back into the stomach
- the **glottis** closes, and the soft palate raises to stop vomit entering the airways
- abdominal pressure squeezes the stomach, forcing its contents back through the oesophagus and out through the mouth.

Vomiting is the body's mechanism for getting rid of harmful substances – protecting it from poisons and infected foods. Too much vomiting can itself be damaging, though, leading to a dangerous loss of fluids and salts.

# SMALL INTESTINE

The small intestine lies between the stomach and the large intestine. In an adult, it is about 3–4 centimetres in diameter; its total length is more than 6 metres but muscles in the intestinal wall usually keep it contracted to about half this length. It is subdivided into three main areas: the duodenum, jejunum and ileum. Food remains in the small intestine for between 1 and 6 hours. **Digestion** of food and absorption of **nutrients** takes place within the small intestine, leaving mainly waste matter to pass into the large intestine.

When the **chyme** leaves the stomach, it passes into the duodenum. This is about 25 centimetres long, and is shaped like the letter 'C'. In the duodenum, digestive juices from the liver and **pancreas** are added to the chyme:
- **bile** is a watery, **alkaline** fluid made by the liver and stored in the gall bladder. It does not contain any **enzymes**, but bile salts act on **fats** to break them up into small droplets.
- pancreatic juice from the pancreas contains several enzymes. Proteases break down **proteins** into peptides and **amino acids**. Pancreatic amylase digests starch, converting it into maltose. Lipase digests fats, breaking them down into **fatty acids** and **glycerol**. These enzymes do not work well in an acidic environment, so pancreatic juice also contains an alkali to neutralize the **acid** chyme.

liver

stomach

gall bladder
bile duct
duodenum

pancreas

This diagram shows the duodenum and its connections with the bile duct.

This photomicrograph shows the finger-like villi in part of the small intestine wall.

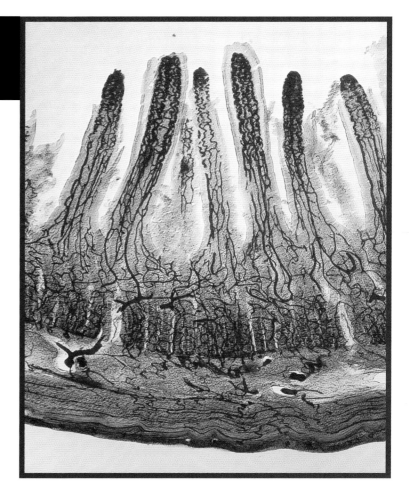

From the duodenum, the chyme passes into the jejunum (about 2.5 metres long) and then into the ileum (about 3.5 metres long). Glands in the walls of the small intestine produce a dilute **mucus** and salt solution for lubrication, and to provide a watery environment for the rest of the digestive processes to take place. Digestive enzymes are also produced by glands (called 'crypts of Lieberkuhn') in the small intestine wall. These enzymes complete the breakdown of peptides into amino acids, and **carbohydrates** into simple sugars.

## Absorbing nutrients

Once food has been digested, it has to be absorbed into the body, and the inner surface of the small intestine is well adapted to do this. **Peristaltic** waves, from the action of muscles in the intestine wall, move the food along through the small intestine. The inner surface area of the **mucosa** has large, circular folds, each covered with tiny projections called 'villi'. Each villus is about 0.5 millimetres long and contains blood **capillaries** and a lymph vessel (a drainage tube, also called a 'lacteal'). The outer edge of each villus is covered with thousands of smaller projections called microvilli. The folds, villi and microvilli, increase the surface area of the small intestine – providing about 600 times greater surface for absorption of nutrients than a flat surface would provide. The walls of each villus are very thin, so that nutrient **molecules** can pass through them, mainly by the process of **diffusion**. Amino acids pass from the villus into the blood capillaries, and are carried away in the bloodstream. Fatty acids pass into the lacteal, and are carried away into the **lymphatic system**. Water and **minerals** are also absorbed into the bloodstream – **water-soluble vitamins** enter the bloodstream and **fat-soluble** vitamins enter the lymphatic system.

After the absorption of nutrients, only waste matter and water is left. This passes into the large intestine.

# LARGE INTESTINE

Liquid waste, from which **nutrients** have been absorbed, enters the large intestine. Water is removed in the large intestine and solid waste passes on to the rectum where it is stored until we go to the toilet.

The large intestine is 1–1.5 metres long – one sixth of the length of the small intestine. It is called the large intestine because it is about 6 centimetres in diameter, whereas the small intestine is less than 4 centimetres in diameter. Its main sections curve round to form the four sides of a rectangle, surrounding the small intestine.

## Caecum

Liquid waste passes into the first section, the caecum, through a **valve** called the ileocaecal **sphincter**. This is usually partly closed, allowing liquid through in a slow, steady trickle. The caecum is a short cul-de-sac, and its open end merges with the next section of the large intestine, the colon. Attached to the caecum is a small narrow tube, the appendix; this does not play any part in **digestion** but may have some function as part of the body's **immune system**.

## Colon

The next section of the large intestine is called the colon. The wall of the large intestine has no villi or folds, and no **enzymes** are produced. Absorptive cells absorb water from the waste, and goblet cells produce **mucus** for lubrication – helping waste slide easily along the large intestine. Liquid waste is continuously pushed along the colon by slow **peristaltic** waves, between three and twelve each minute. The muscular walls of the colon generate these waves. Additionally, three or four times a day, usually during or after a meal, an extra strong peristaltic wave sweeps along the colon, forcing the contents into the rectum.

In this coloured X-ray, the large intestine is shown in yellow. The caecum (left) leads to the colon (centre and left) making a u-shaped loop.

This diagram shows how the main sections of the large intestine are curved into a rectangular shape.

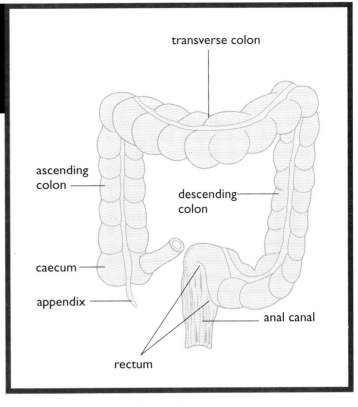

Although we generally think of **bacteria** as being harmful, we rely on the bacteria that live in the large intestine to complete the breakdown of waste. They convert any remaining **carbohydrates** and **proteins** into simpler substances, and release some gases. **Vitamins** K and B12 are by-products of the action of bacteria, and are absorbed into the blood.

## Waste

Solid waste is called **faeces**. It contains water, some **minerals**, waste products from blood and the intestinal walls, bacteria and bacterial products, unabsorbed material and indigestible material such as fibre. An S-shaped bend leads from the end of the colon into the rectum. As faeces collects in the rectum, the rectal walls stretch, stimulating stretch receptors in the wall. Rectal muscles contract, shortening the rectum and increasing the pressure inside. The faeces pass into the anal canal, which has a rich network of blood vessels. At the end of the anal canal is the **anus**, ending in two sphincter muscles, both of which are usually closed. When we go to the toilet, voluntary contraction of the diaphragm and abdominal muscles open the sphincters and faeces is pushed out of the body through the anus.

### Appendicitis

Any blockage in the appendix can lead to inflammation that we call appendicitis. It usually causes an uncomfortable feeling in the abdomen, which becomes severe. A hundred years ago, appendicitis was rare. Doctors think that it is becoming increasingly common because our diet generally contains much less fibre than that of previous generations. An operation to remove the appendix is usually carried out, to prevent the risk of the appendix bursting and spreading infection inside the abdomen. Because the appendix does not carry out any important function, we can live quite happily without it.

# INTESTINAL PROBLEMS

Everybody has probably experienced an intestinal problem at some time. Some problems are mild and pass quickly, while others are more serious and may be long lasting.

This hand print shows the bacteria that can develop if we do not wash our hands!

## Diarrhoea

If waste moves through the large intestine too quickly, water cannot be absorbed. This results in watery **faeces** and the uncontrollable need to go to the toilet urgently. Diarrhoea may be caused by infection from **bacteria** or a **virus**, often a result of eating food infected with a bacterium such as salmonella. It can also be caused by toxic substances, such as some weed killers, and sometimes by extreme nervousness.

Diarrhoea that continues for some time can lead to dehydration and loss of salts because they pass through the alimentary canal too quickly to be absorbed. This is not usually serious in adults, but can be very dangerous in young children.

High standards of hygiene, both in food preparation and in personal behaviour, such as washing your hands after using the toilet, can help to reduce the risk of diarrhoea from bacterial infection.

## Constipation

If waste moves through the large intestine too slowly, too much water may be absorbed from it. This results in hard faeces and difficulty in **defecation**. Constipation may be caused by a variety of factors, including a lack of fibre in the diet, too little exercise, stress and some drugs. A mild laxative, which speeds up the movement of waste through the large intestine, may help to relieve the problem.

## Inflammatory diseases

The intestine may become inflamed, giving a cramping pain and fever. If the inflammation is just in the large intestine, it is called ulcerative colitis; if it extends to other places in the alimentary canal, especially the ileum, it may be called Crohn's disease. A single cause has not been proved, but doctors think it may be due to an infection or **food allergy**. In mild cases, simple diarrhoea remedies and **vitamin** supplements may be all that is needed. In more serious cases, drugs such as steroids may be given to suppress the **immune system**. Surgery to remove part of the bowel may be necessary.

## Irritable Bowel Syndrome

People suffering from irritable bowel syndrome (IBS) have alternating bouts of diarrhoea and constipation, together with abdominal cramps and pains, and a feeling of sickness and loss of appetite. This condition is often associated with stress and depression. A change of diet, to include more fibre, can sometimes help, and some drugs are available to help to control the symptoms.

This photograph shows part of an intestine affected by Crohn's disease, which can seriously affect the digestive system.

## Hernia

A hernia is a lump that arises when a loop of intestine protrudes through the abdominal wall lining. They are common, and may be due to an inborn weakness, a serious, persistent cough (such as whooping cough or bronchitis) or the strain of lifting heavy objects. Hernias may be treated by surgical repair or by the wearing of a special belt.

## Haemorrhoids

Commonly called 'piles', these are swellings that arise inside the anal canal. They are spongy tissues with a rich supply of blood vessels. As they get larger, they lead to bleeding and can be painful. The discomfort can be eased by a warm bath, and a high fibre diet makes defecation easier. Treatment can be by injection to make the haemorrhoids shrivel, by freezing them, or by restricting their blood supply. An operation may sometimes be necessary to remove them completely.

## Bowel cancer

Bowel cancer has become increasingly common, and many doctors think this is because our diets contain less fibre and more animal **fat** than in the past. It may cause diarrhoea or constipation, bleeding from the rectum and dull pain. If diagnosed in the early stages, many patients can be cured.

The liver is the largest organ in the body, with a mass of about 1.5 kilograms. It lies just below the diaphragm, a sheet of muscle that separates the chest from the abdomen. The liver has two lobes, the right (which is six times bigger than the left) lies in front of the right kidney. The liver is involved in the regulation and control of many of the body's systems.

## Inside the liver

The liver is made up of many small areas called lobules. Each lobule has five or six sides, and is about 1 millimetre in diameter. Blood and **bile** flow through the lobules in opposite directions.

## Blood supply

Blood is brought to the liver in the **hepatic artery** and hepatic portal **vein**. The liver does not contain blood **capillaries**, but each lobule has a series of spaces, through which the blood passes. Liver cells take up oxygen, **nutrients** and toxic substances. The blood picks up products made by the liver and nutrients to be transported elsewhere in the body.

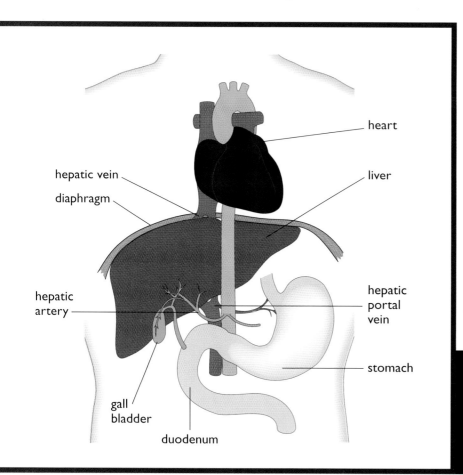

- heart
- liver
- hepatic vein
- diaphragm
- hepatic artery
- hepatic portal vein
- stomach
- gall bladder
- duodenum

## What does the liver do?

The conditions inside our bodies, such as temperature, chemical levels and water level, need to be kept constant. The regulation of this internal environment is called homeostasis, and most of it is carried out by the liver.

This diagram shows the position of the liver in the body, and the blood vessels and organs that surround it.

The main functions of the liver include:

- regulation of blood sugar levels (the concentration of sugar in the blood): when the blood sugar level is high, the liver removes **glucose** from the blood and stores it as **glycogen**. When the blood sugar level drops, the reverse happens.
- **fat** metabolism: the liver breaks down **fatty acids** and builds up new substances from them. Every day, the liver produces about 1 litre of bile, which is essential for the **digestion** of fats in the small intestine.

Here, you can see a lobule of the liver – greatly magnified.

- **protein** metabolism: when **amino acids** are broken down, ammonia is produced; this is toxic, and so the liver converts it into a harmless chemical, urea, which is excreted in urine. The liver also produces some amino acids and proteins that are needed in the blood.
- **vitamins**: the liver **synthesises** vitamin A from carotene, a chemical found in some fruits and vegetables, especially carrots. The liver also activates vitamin D and stores many other vitamins until they are needed.
- **minerals**: the liver removes iron from the **haemoglobin** of broken down red blood cells, and stores it until it can be used to make new red blood cells; haemoglobin is vital for the transport of oxygen. The liver also stores other minerals until they are needed.
- toxins: harmful chemicals such as alcohol, drugs, poisons, environmental pollutants and surplus **hormones** are removed from the blood and broken down by **enzymes** in the liver
- temperature control: the many chemical reactions that are carried out inside the liver generate heat. This warms the blood as it passes through, and the blood carries the heat to the rest of the body, helping to maintain a constant body temperature.

## Gall bladder

The gall bladder is a small, pear-shaped organ that lies under a lobe of the liver. It stores bile and makes it more concentrated by absorbing water from it. The gall bladder also produces **mucus** for lubrication.

The liver is a complex organ, continuously carrying out a large variety of chemical reactions. It carries out vital functions without which the body would not survive, but it can be damaged by poisons, drugs and infections.

## Cirrhosis

This is a chronic liver disease, in that normal liver cells are destroyed and replaced by fibrous tissue that makes the liver hard and unable to function efficiently. In the early stages there may be no symptoms, but as the disease progresses **hormones** may accumulate as the liver fails to break them down, and **jaundice** may occur as **bile** builds up in the blood. The abdomen may swell, body muscles become weak, and there may be internal bleeding. Eventually the circulation in the liver is blocked, leading to liver failure and death. The most common cause of cirrhosis is heavy consumption of alcohol over a long period of time. The liver is, however, able to repair itself, provided it is not too badly damaged. If cirrhosis is detected at an early stage, and the patient stops drinking alcohol, the damage can be repaired.

## Hepatitis

Hepatitis is usually caused by a viral infection, resulting in inflammation of the liver. It can affect people of all ages and is highly infectious. There are three main types: A, B and C.

Hepatitis A is often spread in contaminated food or water. It is usually a mild disease, causing no long-term problems.

Fibrous scar tissue (green) has developed around the lobules in this patient's liver. This damage has been caused by too much alcohol.

Hepatitis B and Hepatitis C may be spread in infected blood, and they can also be spread sexually. They are common among drug addicts who may share hypodermic needles. Babies of infected pregnant women may also be infected.

In most cases, infection by Hepatitis A or B is mild and may not even be noticed although blood tests can detect the infection and indicate which **virus** is involved. More severe infections can result in jaundice, with recovery within a few weeks. In some cases, the infection persists and the liver is permanently damaged.

Treatment of hepatitis includes rest and a diet rich in **carbohydrates**, but low in **fat**.

## Jaundice

When old red blood cells are broken down and the yellow bile pigment is released, it is usually removed from the blood by the liver. It is then **excreted** from the liver in bile, and the levels of bile pigment in the

This X-ray shows that the patient's gall bladder (red, pear-shaped) contains many gallstones (green).

blood are normally very low. If the amounts in the blood rise, the skin becomes a yellow colour and the patient may feel more tired than usual. This is known as jaundice and it is common in newborn babies, when the liver is not mature enough to cope with the breakdown of red blood cells.

## Gallstones

If there is too much cholesterol (fatty substance) in the bile, or not enough bile salts, the cholesterol may crystallize, forming gallstones. Initially, these may not cause any problems, but as they get bigger they may block the bile duct. Bile cannot leave the gall bladder, so fat **digestion** is impaired and jaundice may occur. In some cases, eating a fat-free diet can control the problem. Alternatively, gallstones can be treated with drugs to dissolve them or by lithotripsy (shockwaves) to shatter them. They may also be surgically removed and in some patients the entire gall bladder may be removed. After treatment, the patient can resume a perfectly normal life.

# PANCREAS

Just behind the stomach lies a small, pinkish-grey organ called the **pancreas**. This produces pancreatic juice containing important digestive **enzymes**. It also produces **hormones**, including **insulin** and **glycogen** that help to regulate the amount of sugar in the blood.

In an adult, the pancreas is about 12–15 centimetres long and 2.5 centimetres thick. The cells of the pancreas need a good blood supply to allow them to function and to carry away the hormones they produce.

When taste buds in the mouth detect food, messages are sent to the brain; in turn, the brain sends messages to the pancreas, stimulating the production of pancreatic juice in preparation for **digestion** of the food.

Here, you can see how the cells inside the pancreas are arranged in an islet of Langerhans.

The majority of cells in the pancreas are exocrine cells, seen here – greatly magnified.

## Pancreatic cells

There are two main types of cell in the pancreas, exocrine cells and endocrine cells.

About 99 per cent of the pancreatic cells are exocrine cells. These are arranged in groups, and they produce pancreatic juice. They are clustered together around tiny ducts, which form a network to carry the pancreatic juice away. These ducts eventually join together to form two large ducts. The bigger of these is the pancreatic duct. This joins the common **bile** duct from the gall bladder and liver, and carries pancreatic juice and bile to the duodenum (part of the small intestine). The smaller of the two ducts is the accessory duct, which leads straight from the pancreas into the duodenum, about 2–3 centimetres higher than the pancreatic duct.

The other 1 per cent of cells in the pancreas are endocrine cells. These cells are clustered together into small groups called islets of Langerhans. There are four different types of cell in each islet, each producing a different hormone that is released into the blood.

These hormones interact with each other, and this interaction helps to regulate the amounts of each that are produced. Blood components and intestinal contents also play a part in regulating the production of these hormones.

There are several types of diabetes, all of which lead to the inability to control blood sugar levels. It is a major cause of death in developed countries, more because of its side effects than the disorder itself.

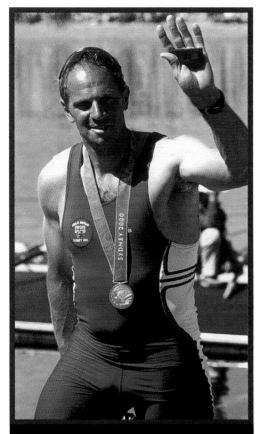

As long as it is properly monitored, there is no reason why diabetes should stop anyone taking part in sport.

## Controlling blood sugar levels

Blood sugar levels are controlled by the interaction of the liver and **pancreas**.

The pancreas produces **hormones, insulin** and **glycogen**. If the level of sugar in the blood begins to drop, the pancreas produces glycogen. This enters the blood and is carried to the liver, where it stimulates liver cells to convert some of their stored glycogen into **glucose**. This is released into the blood, and the blood sugar level climbs back to normal.

If the amount of sugar in the blood rises above normal, the pancreas produces insulin. It enters the blood and is carried to the liver where it stimulates liver cells to remove glucose from the blood and store it as glycogen. This reduces the blood sugar level.

This feedback system operates effectively to maintain the blood sugar level within the correct limits. In patients with diabetes, the system does not operate and they are therefore unable to control their blood sugar levels.

## Types of diabetes

There are two main types of diabetes:
* *Type I (insulin-dependent)*
  This usually begins before the age of 20, and continues throughout the rest of the patient's life. One of the main causes is the **immune system** attacking and destroying the cells in the pancreas, preventing insulin production. Excess glucose builds up in the blood and is **excreted** in the urine; the patient may produce up to 20 litres of urine a day, and needs to drink a lot of water to replace this fluid. The body behaves as if it is starving. Waste products called ketones build up in the blood and make the blood more acidic – if untreated, this may eventually cause death. Regular injections of insulin, to compensate for sugar intake, prevent this happening.

Side effects of Type I diabetes include weight loss, heart and blood problems, loss of vision and kidney damage.

- *Type II (non-insulin dependent)*
  Type II diabetes accounts for 90 per cent of diabetics. It usually affects overweight people over the age of 35. Patients have plenty of insulin, but their cells have become less sensitive to it. The symptoms are milder than those of Type I; some patients may need insulin injections, but in many the high glucose levels are controllable by a low-sugar diet, regular exercise and weight loss.

Other types of diabetes are less common and may have a variety of causes.

## Hyperinsulinism (also called hypoglycaemia)

This can occur if a patient injects too much insulin. The blood sugar level falls too low, and brain cells do not have enough glucose to function normally. Within minutes, the patient feels shaky and, unless glucose is given quickly, will become unconscious and may die.

Type I diabetics lack insulin so they need to inject it regularly.

## Hyperglycaemia

Hyperglycaemia can occur if a patient's blood sugar level rises too high. It is a much slower process than hypoglycaemia, taking several hours to develop, and several hours to get back to normal.

### Living with diabetes

Although the outlook for diabetics has improved dramatically, it is still not an easy condition to live with. Controlling the blood sugar level requires careful discipline and this can be very frustrating, especially if you are a teenager just wanting to be the same as your friends. A dietician can help you plan what to eat and what to avoid – reducing **fats**, avoiding sugar and salt, and eating regular meals are all important. The amount of food you take in must be carefully balanced with the amount of exercise that you do. Doctors will give instructions about how often the blood or urine should be tested to show the sugar levels, and about how much insulin must be injected and how often.

We have two kidneys, which are reddish organs, each about 10–12 centimetres long and about 5 centimetres wide. They lie one on each side of the spine just above the waist and are partly protected by the lower ribs. The right kidney is a little lower than the left, because the liver takes up some abdominal space on the right of the body. Their main function is to filter the blood, removing waste chemicals and water, and producing a liquid, called urine, which is passed to the bladder. Having filtered out unwanted chemicals, the kidneys then pass back salts, other chemicals and water to the blood, ensuring that the right level of each is maintained.

## Blood supply

In order to filter the blood, the kidneys need a good blood supply. Blood travels to each kidney via the **renal arteries** and leaves via the renal **veins**. Inside the kidney, the arteries branch many times to form a network of smaller vessels. Approximately 1.2 litres of blood flows through the kidneys every minute – all the blood in the body passes through the kidneys about 340 times every day!

Together, the kidneys are able to filter more blood than the body actually needs them to. A single kidney is able to filter enough blood on its own. We can survive and live a healthy, active life with just one kidney.

We have two kidneys, one on either side of the spine, above the waist.

This diagram shows the internal structure of a kidney.

## Kidney structure

Each kidney has a transparent outer membrane that anchors it to the abdominal wall. Below this is a layer of **fat** that acts as a cushion to protect the kidney from damage.

If a kidney is cut in half from top to bottom, three different areas can be seen:

- at the centre of the kidney is a large space called the pelvis. This is where urine collects. The pelvis is connected to a narrow tube called a ureter, along which urine flows from the kidney to the bladder.
- the middle part of the kidney is a pale area called the medulla. This is made up of 8–18 cone shaped areas, and contains ducts that carry urine to the pelvis.
- the darker outer layer, the cortex, is where the blood is filtered. Here, the renal arteries branch into smaller vessels called arterioles. Each arteriole leads to a glomerulus, a group of blood vessels coiled round into a knot. Around each glomerulus is a renal capsule (sometimes called a Bowman's capsule) leading to a renal tubule. These eventually join collecting ducts that pass through the medulla, opening into the pelvis at the top of a pyramid shape. The cortex of a kidney contains thousands of glomeruli. One glomerulus, with its renal capsule, tubule and blood **capillaries** is called a nephron.

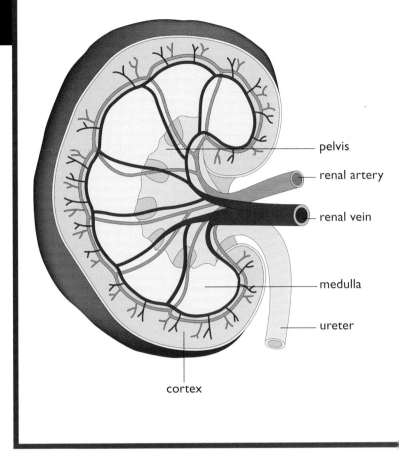

pelvis
renal artery
renal vein
medulla
ureter
cortex

## Kidney transplant

A patient's diseased kidney may be removed and replaced with a healthy one from another person. Drugs need to be taken to ensure that the patient's body does not reject the new kidney. Unfortunately, the waiting list for kidneys is long and patients may wait many years before a suitable kidney becomes available.

# WHAT HAPPENS IN THE KIDNEYS?

A nephron consists of a single glomerulus together with its blood **capillaries**, **renal** capsule and renal tubule. It is here that the basic functions of the kidney are carried out. Blood is filtered, unwanted substances are removed and useful substances are returned to the blood. This maintains the correct levels of fluid and chemicals in the blood and produces urine, so that waste can leave the body.

## Ultra-filtration

The glomerulus and its capillaries are the places where ultra-filtration occurs. This is the process by which substances are removed from the blood.

Blood enters the glomerulus via a capillary. The capillary leaving the glomerulus is narrower than the one entering it, so the pressure inside the glomerulus is raised. This forces fluid out of the blood through the capillary wall. Blood cells and plasma **proteins** are retained, as they are too large to pass through the capillary wall. The fluid that passes out

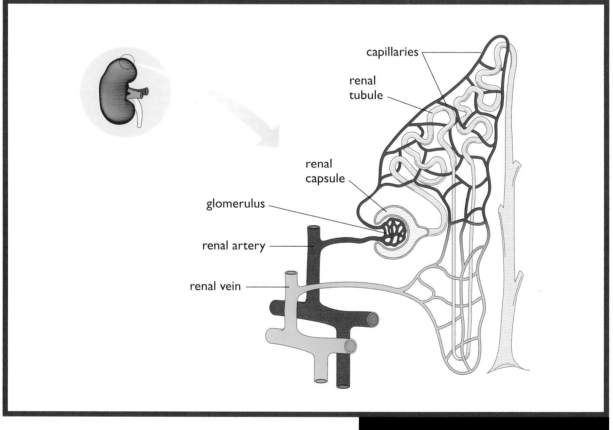

These pictures show what the internal structure of a kidney is like, when magnified.

by **diffusion** is mainly water and dissolved salts, **glucose**, urea and uric **acid**. This fluid collects in the renal capsule.

## Selective reabsorption

Selective reabsorption is the process by which substances are added back to the blood. It takes place as the fluid collected in the renal capsule trickles down the renal tubule.

As the fluid flows through the tubule, substances that the body needs are absorbed back into the blood. Water, glucose and some salts are taken back, to maintain the correct levels in the blood. The fluid then passes through the collecting duct and eventually to the pelvis of the kidney, before it leaves the kidney via the ureter.

## Urine production

Any water and salts not needed by the body pass on down the tubule, together with urea and uric acid. They enter the renal tubule, and collect in the pelvis of the kidney, forming the liquid we call urine.

## Urine tests

Urine can contain different amounts of different substances and this can provide important information about your health. Too much glucose in the urine can be a sign of diabetes, while the presence of protein in urine may be a sign of kidney failure. Pregnancy tests detect a **hormone** (human chorionic gonadotrophin, HCG) that is produced by a fertilized egg, and **excreted** in the mother's urine within a couple of weeks of conception.

> ### How much urine?
> Normally, we produce about 1–1.5 litres of urine every day. This is affected by the amount of water we drink, and the amount that we sweat. If we drink a lot, we produce a lot of urine. The amount of chemicals to be filtered out remains the same, so the urine is very dilute. If we sweat a lot, we produce much less urine. Again, there is still the same amount of chemicals to be filtered out, so the urine is more concentrated. Some substances, such as caffeine and alcohol, are diuretics – they increase the amount of urine produced. Dilute urine is a very pale, almost colourless liquid. The more concentrated it is, the darker and stronger the colour.

# KIDNEY PROBLEMS

There are a variety of things that can affect the efficient functioning of the kidneys. Some problems may affect just one kidney, while other problems may affect both. If one kidney fails, the other is usually able to cope with the extra work. If both fail, a patient has to rely on mechanical methods to clean the blood.

## Kidney stones

These are formed when crystals of salts present in urine solidify into **insoluble** lumps. If they settle in narrow tubes, such as the ureters, they can cause violent, stabbing pains. Kidney stones can be surgically removed, but a newer, alternative technique for their removal is 'shock wave lithotripsy'. This involves brief, high-intensity sound waves fired at the stones, eventually shattering them into tiny fragments which are carried away in the urine.

## Bacterial infections

Bacterial infections can affect any of the tissues of the kidneys. They are most commonly caused by **bacteria** such as *Escherichia coli* (*E.coli*), a bacterium that is usually present in the intestines, spreading from the bladder to the ureters and then into the kidneys. Treatment with **antibiotics** usually brings the infection under control quickly.

This is a photograph of E.coli, which can cause kidney infections.

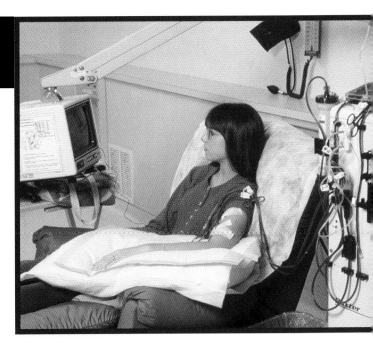

This girl has kidney failure and is using a dialysis machine to cleanse her blood.

## Cancer of the kidney

This is much more common in men than in women, and occurs most often between the ages of 50 and 60. If detected in the early stages, treatment may be by surgery to remove the kidney, followed by **radiotherapy** and **chemotherapy**. However, the cancer often spreads to other parts of the body, making treatment less successful.

## Floating kidney

If a kidney is not attached to the back of the abdomen, it is free to move around inside the abdomen – this is called a 'floating kidney'. It can be caused by sudden wrenching movements, and it may twist the ureter, making it difficult or impossible to pass urine.

## Kidney defects

Some people are born with kidney defects. These include having only one kidney, two kidneys fused together, two ureters from each kidney, cysts inside the kidneys and kidneys in the wrong place within the abdomen. Each individual case is different; some may need treatment while others will not cause any problems and may be unnoticed for years.

## Kidney failure

This may be sudden (acute), or slowly develop over several years (chronic). There are a variety of causes, including heart attack, build-up of toxic chemicals, kidney blockage and kidney inflammation. A wide range of symptoms may be seen, but the main symptom is a significant reduction in the amount of urine produced.

### Treating kidney failure: dialysis

Blood must still be cleansed, and if a patient's kidneys are unable to perform the task, a dialysis machine (or 'artificial kidney') may be used. This pumps blood from an **artery** through a series of tubes made from an absorbent membrane. A solution called dialysis fluid is on the other side of the membrane, and as blood passes along, the salts and waste products move out of the blood by **diffusion**, through the membrane and into the dialysis fluid. The cleansed blood then goes back to the body. Each cycle of dialysis takes several hours, and most patients need treatment two or three times every week.

The bladder is a sac that collects urine from the kidneys and holds it until we go to the toilet. Urine contains waste products and urination is an efficient method of removing them from the body.

## Ureters

The ureters are narrow tubes that carry urine from the kidneys to the bladder. Each ureter is between 25–30 centimetres long, and between 1–10 millimetres in diameter. Urine is forced along the ureters by **peristaltic** waves, one to five times every minute depending on how fast urine is being produced.

The ureters enter the bladder, one at each side. Before they open to the inside of the bladder, they run at an oblique (slanted) angle for a short distance as they pass through the bladder wall; this acts as a check valve, allowing urine to flow into the bladder but preventing it from flowing backwards.

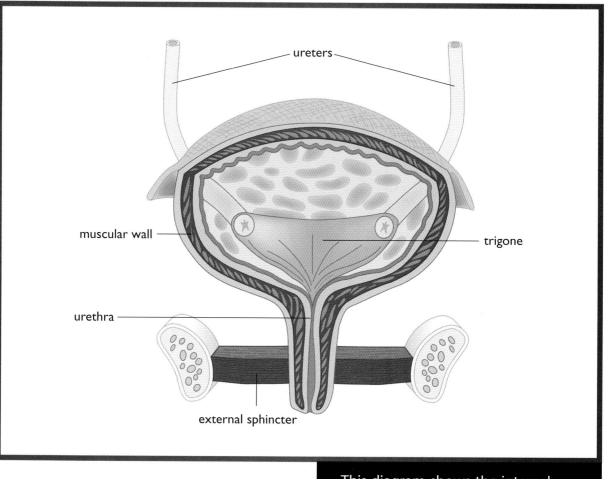

This diagram shows the internal structure of the bladder.

## Bladder

The bladder is a hollow, stretchy organ, held in place by the folds of the **peritoneum**. Its shape depends on how much urine it contains: if it is empty, it is collapsed, like an empty balloon; when partly full, it is spherical; when completely full, it is pear-shaped.

## Urethra

The urethra is a tube of smooth muscle that carries urine from the bladder to outside the body. It is about 4 centimetres long in a female, running from the bladder and opening just in front of the vagina. In males, the urethra is about 20 centimetres long, running from the bladder along the length of the penis, to open at the tip of the penis. A ring of muscle around the urethra (a **sphincter**) controls the release of urine from the body.

## Urination

On average, an adult's bladder can hold 700–800 millilitres of urine, but we usually feel more comfortable emptying it when it is about half-full. When the bladder contains 300–400 millilitres of urine, the pressure inside it increases. Stretch receptors in the bladder wall send signals to the spinal cord, triggering a reflex reaction. This makes muscles in the bladder wall contract, and the urethral sphincter relaxes. Urine is forced out of the bladder and through the urethra.

As children, we learn to control this reflex and can delay urination for a limited period.

## Incontinence

In young children, incontinence is normal because they have not learned to control the reflex reaction. Adults may also suffer from incontinence too, often as a result of physical stresses – coughing, sneezing, laughing, exercising and pregnancy can all increase abdominal pressure and cause leakage from the bladder. It can also be caused by physical injury, ageing, disease and the effects of some drugs.

### Cystitis

This is inflammation of the bladder. It is usually caused by the **bacterium** *Escherichia coli* (E.coli), and is much more common in women than in men. The first sign is a tingling or burning sensation when urinating, which gradually gets worse and more painful. Treatment may be with **antibiotics** to kill the bacteria. Drinking plenty of water, a healthy diet and good personal hygiene can all help to reduce the likelihood of cystitis occurring.

# WHAT CAN GO WRONG WITH MY DIGESTIVE SYSTEM?

This book has explained the different parts of the digestive system, why it is important and how it can be damaged by injury and illness. This page summarizes some of the problems that can affect young people. It also gives you information about how each problem is treated.

Many problems can also be avoided by good health behaviour. This is called prevention. Taking regular exercise and getting plenty of rest are important, as is eating a balanced diet. A balanced diet is particularly important for maintaining a healthy digestive system. The table tells you some of the ways you can prevent injury and illness.

Remember, if you think something is wrong with your body, you should always talk to a trained medical professional, like a doctor or a school nurse. Regular medical check-ups are an important part of maintaining a healthy body.

| Illness or injury | Cause | Symptoms | Prevention | Treatment |
|---|---|---|---|---|
| Tooth decay | Damage to teeth by acid from **bacteria** in the mouth. | Toothache, mild at first but developing to severe pain if untreated. | Calcium-rich diet e.g. plenty of milk. Avoid sweets and sugary foods and drinks. Maintain good dental hygiene, brushing and flossing teeth twice a day. Have regular dental check-ups. | Cleaning of tooth and drilling out damaged tooth tissue. Replacement with plastic or metal material. In severe cases, removal of the tooth may be necessary. |
| Indigestion | Overeating, eating too quickly, eating particular foods such as curry, cucumber or onion. Stress. | Pain after a meal, and a bloated, sick feeling. | Eat smaller meals, eat more slowly and avoid foods that are likely to cause indigestion. Reduce stress. | Being sick gets rid of excess or problem food. Antacid tablets can reduce the acidity of the stomach contents. |

| Illness or injury | Cause | Symptoms | Prevention | Treatment |
|---|---|---|---|---|
| Diarrhoea | Bacterial and **viral** infection, toxic substances such as weedkiller. Extreme nervousness. | Watery **faeces**. An uncontrollable need to go to the toilet urgently. | Maintain high standards of personal hygiene, such as always washing hands after using the toilet. Prepare and store food hygienically. | Drink water to replace lost fluid. **Antibiotics** may help to clear up an infection. Ingestion of toxic substances may require urgent medical treatment. |
| Irritable Bowel Syndrome | Stress or depression. Lack of fibre in the diet. | Bouts of diarrhoea and constipation, abdominal cramps and pains, sickness, loss of appetite. | Reduce stress. Change diet to include more fibre by eating more fruit and vegetables. | Some drugs can help to control the symptoms. |
| Constipation | Too little exercise. Stress. Lack of fibre in the diet. | Hard faeces, making it difficult to go to the toilet. | Increase exercise and reduce stress. Change diet to include more fibre by eating more fruit and vegetables. | A mild laxative can help to move waste through the large intestine more quickly, easing the problem. |

## Further reading

*Horrible Science, Disgusting Digestion*, Nick Arnold, Tony de Saules (Scholastic Hippo, 1998)
*The Human Machine, The Food Processor: All about your digestive system*, Sarah Angliss (Belitha Press, 1999)
*Human Physiology and Health*, David Wright (Heinemann Educational, 2000)
*Look at Your Body, Digestion*, Steve Parker (Franklin Watts, 1996)

# GLOSSARY

**acid** liquid that is sour to taste, can eat away metals and is neutralized by alkalis and bases

**alkali** opposite of acid

**amino acid** one of the basic units of a protein molecule

**anaemia** lack of haemoglobin in the blood

**antibiotics** drug used to destroy harmful bacteria and fungi

**anus** opening through which solid waste leaves the body

**artery** large blood vessel carrying blood away from the heart

**bacteria** group of micro-organisms that can cause infections

**bile** liquid produced by the liver that helps to break down fats

**bolus** lump of food that is swallowed

**capillary** very fine blood vessel that links arteries and veins

**carbohydrate** nutrient that can be broken down to release energy

**chemotherapy** treatment of disease, especially cancer, by the use of chemical substances

**chyme** partly-digested liquid food that leaves the stomach

**circular muscles** muscles arranged in rings

**defecation** removal of solid waste from the body

**diffusion** movement of molecules from an area of high concentration to an area of low concentration

**digestion** process of breaking food down into smaller units

**enzyme** protein that acts as a catalyst in (speeds up) chemical reactions

**excrete** to get rid of waste substances

**faeces** solid waste material that leaves the body

**fat** substance that stores and releases energy

**fat-soluble** can be dissolved in oils

**fatty acid** one of the basic units of a fat molecule

**food allergy** sensitivity to a particular food that may lead to an allergic reaction

**gastric** to do with the stomach

**glottis** space between the vocal cords at the top of the larynx

**glucose** sugar that stores and releases energy

**glycerol** substance that combines with fatty acids to make fats

**glycogen** sugar that can be stored by the body

**haemoglobin** red pigment found in red blood cells , which transports oxygen around the body

**hepatic** to do with the liver

**hormones** chemicals made in the body. They travel around the body in the blood and affect organs and tissues in a variety of ways.

**immune system** body's defence mechanisms against infection and disease

**insoluble** will not dissolve

**insulin** hormone produced by the pancreas

**jaundice** condition where the skin turns yellowish as excess bile pigments build up in the blood

**longitudinal muscles** muscles that run straight up and down

**lymphatic system** system of drainage vessels, also involved in the body's immune responses

**mineral** one of a number of chemicals needed by the body in very small amounts, e.g. calcium and iron

**molecules** tiny particles of a chemical

**mucosa** layer of tissue that produces mucus

**mucus** sticky, slimy fluid that acts as a lubricant

**nutrient** part of our food that the body can use

**pancreas** abdominal organ that produces insulin and other hormones

**peristalsis** wave motion of muscles that pushes food along the alimentary canal

**peritoneum** membrane lining the abdominal cavity and covering the organs within it

**protein** type of large molecule that makes up some of the basic structures of all living things

**radiotherapy** treatment of disease, especially cancer, by the use of X-rays or similar radiation

**renal** to do with the kidneys

**saliva** digestive juice made by salivary glands in the mouth

**soluble** able to dissolve in a liquid

**sphincter** ring of muscle that closes an opening

**synthesis** making something new

**valve** mechanism for controlling the flow of a liquid through a tube

**vein** large blood vessel carrying blood back to the heart

**virus** very small micro-organism that can cause infection

**vitamin** one of a number of complex chemicals that the body needs

**water-soluble** can be dissolved in water

# INDEX